BOSTON

A PICTURE BOOK TO REMEMBER HER BY

Designed by
DAVID GIBBON

Produced by
TED SMART

CRESCENT

INTRODUCTION

The city of Boston occupies a significant position in the development of America as a whole, for its history and the history of the U.S. began almost simultaneously and many of the events central to the formation of America as it is today took place in and around this early settlement. In 1630, only ten years after the Pilgrims landed at Plymouth, Boston was founded by Puritan Englishmen of the Massachusetts Bay Company, who for religious reasons, put the Atlantic Ocean between themselves and the Church of England and started a settlement which was named after Boston in Lincolnshire, the former home of a number of the immigrants. The settlers looked to the sea for their resources and the marsh-ridden Shawmut Peninsula soon became an important shipbuilding centre and fishing port. It was not long however, before the increasing prosperity of the colonial merchants drew the attention of London to the Massachusetts Bay and the British began pressing for laws to restrict the trading activities of the colonies, which were cutting into their own profits. By the middle of the eighteenth century 'taxation without representation is tyranny' had become the battle cry for revolution among the settlers and after the Boston Massacre of 1770, in which British troops fired on a crowd of civilian hecklers, killing a number of them, the colony was ripe for action. The beginning of this action was marked by the famous Boston Tea Party: in 1773 as a protest against the Tea Act passed by the British Parliament, colonists disguised as Indians dumped three ship-loads of tea into the murky waters of Boston Harbour. On 18th April, 1775 the intrepid Paul Revere made his legendary ride to alert his countrymen that the redcoats were on the march in search of revolutionaries and their leaders, John Hancock and Samuel Adams. Because of this warning, the Minutemen were ready the next morning on Lexington Green for the historic battle that launched the War of Independence. The Battle of Bunker Hill took place on 17th June of that year and by the Autumn, Boston was a military garrison with General George Washington in charge of the Colonial army. The British were ousted and Boston, the settlement that had played so vital a role in the fight for liberty, was set free.

From this point onwards Boston's development was considerable. By the close of the eighteenth century trade, which had suffered initially because British Imperial ports were placed out of bounds, began to pick up and the population swelled to 25,000. The architecture of Charles Bullfinch, who for more than a quarter of a century was also the head of the town government, began to gain international reputation as he set about skilfully transforming an 18th century English town into a 19th century American city and converting the upland pastures of Beacon Hill into a handsome new residential district that has survived to this day with relatively little change. In the 19th century also Boston established itself as a major shipbuilding and manufacturing centre, as well as an important stop on the 'underground railway' via which the Abolitionists smuggled slaves into Canada.

The hilly Shawmut Peninsula to which the settlers had first come had been almost entirely surrounded by water with, to the west, an area of mudflats and marshes which were covered by tides at high water and known collectively as the Back Bay. As pressure of population caused an increasing demand for land however, hills were cut down to fill in coves and gradually so much new land was created that the once water-ringed peninsula became an indistinguishable part of the mainland. Today the original Back Bay is the midtown area (although still called Back Bay), all of South Boston with its docks and marine park is on land reclaimed from the bay; and what was once Noddle Island is now the vast Logan International Airport which has reached out into what was at one time the sea.

Perhaps more than anything else then, it is the lure of history, the fascination of so colourful a development that draws visitors from all over the country and the world to the place where they can follow the path of Paul Revere, visit the shrines where radicals like John Hancock and Samuel Adams incited the colonists to revolution and witness what is the product of the conquest of nature itself. Yet important as the history of Boston may be, there is much more to this city than the memories and monuments of the past. In a way which is almost unique this metropolis of the '70s combines sophistication and 'big-city' excitement with a pace that is positively relaxing. Boston sees itself as a seat of culture, the 'Athens of America' and its citizens are justifiably inordinately proud of the famous Boston Symphony Orchestra, the superb Museum of Fine Arts, of Harvard University and of the prestigious Massachusetts Institute of Technology. It is also a modern city, in which the old is preserved and cherished. Centuries-old meeting houses stand side by side with some of the most modern architecture and grandiose civic projects in the world...all part of contemporary 'New Boston' as epitomized by the Sheraton Boston, the town's most stunning skyscraper hotel and a veritable city within a city. Indeed Boston boasts some of the best hotels in America and countless exciting restaurants serving an amazing variety of seafood for this is 'the seafood capital of the world' and no gourmet could dispute the excellence of the Ipswich clams, Atlantic lobsters, quahog clams and mussels in which the waters off the Massachusetts coast abound. The sea which first brought the settlers to Boston and to which they turned for a livelihood in the early days still plays a significant role in the lives of Bostonians and it is perhaps the timeless waters of the ocean which lend harmony and unity to a city of infinite variety, the dynamic 'Hub of New England'.

Pictured *left* is the New Boston City Hall, by the architects Kallman, McKinnell and Knowles, and *overleaf* can be seen the skyscrapers of downtown Boston as they rise above the Charles River.

From the helicopter *below* can be seen magnificent vistas of the city skyline: downtown Boston is shown *top left* and *bottom left,* with Fenway Park in the foreground, and *centre left* the Quincy Market area. Nestling amid the high-rise buildings *above* is The First Church of Christ Scientist, whilst *right* is pictured the Longfellow Bridge as it spans the Charles River basin between Boston and Cambridge.

The Christian Science Church Center *above and above right* is the World Headquarters of The Mother Church of the First Church of Christ Scientist, and from its precincts can be seen the spectacular 750-foot high Prudential Tower *right and below.* Approached across an eight-acre red brick plaza, the New Boston City Hall *left* was opened in 1969 amid a storm of controversy and dubbed "an Aztec Tomb" by its critics.

Boston's historical background, so closely associated with the sea, is most keenly felt along the waterfront area which is gradually being rejuvenated, as seen *above* near Commercial Wharf, to provide "a small city within a city". It was here, in Colonial days, that the commercial life of the city was centred, for the clipper ship route was a primary source of income as laden ships would sail in and out of her busy wharves. From the deck *below* of The Brig Beaver II *right*, an authentic replica of one of three ships involved in the notorious Boston Tea Party, visitors can relive history by tossing tea-chests overboard, in imitation of the Colonial rebels.

Centre left is shown the Fort Point Channel; *below left* a pleasure craft moored near Northern Avenue; *above left* the downtown skyline from the stern of a cruiser, whilst *overleaf* the Boston skyline rises above the shimmering, silver water of the Inner Harbour.

contrast to the lovely Old State house *right,* with its distinctive tower *low,* are the towering high-rise uctures on Cambridge Street *above* d the glossy John Hancock Building *t,* seen across the peaceful Charles er.

Sited on the northern side of Boston Common *overleaf,* Beacon Hill, with its old brownstone and brick houses retains its 19th century flavour, evidenced in Mt. Vernon Street *below,* and Louisburg Square *above and above left,* whilst the second oldest burial ground in the city, Copp's Hill, is shown *left and right.*

With its lustrous gold dome, the Massachusetts State House *above, right and left,* within which is the famed Hall of Flags containing the battle flags carried by the Massachusetts troops, is the focal point of Beacon Hill. Known as "The Cradle of Liberty", Faneuil Hall *below* on Dock Square, was donated to the people of Boston by the merchant Peter Faneuil, in 1742.

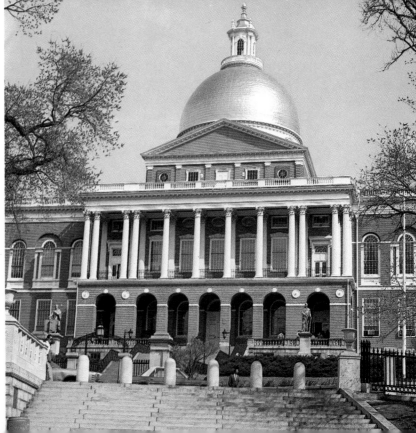

Adjacent to Faneuil Hall, the Quincy Marketplace *these pages* evokes a vivid bazaar-like atmosphere with its banks of flowers and street-level glass-canopied aisles which sell a variety of merchandise.

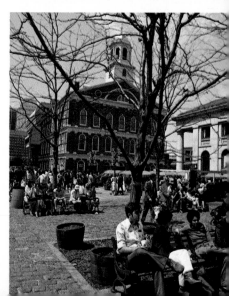

The narrow, cobblestone streets of
Beacon Hill, with their red-brick
sidewalks and gas lamps *these pages*,
are particularly attractive in springtime
and summer when flowering trees and
pretty window boxes enhance the
quaint atmosphere of this historic area,
now designated a National Landmark.

Boston's shopping facilities are justly renowned and the Charles Street neighbourhood, at the foot of Beacon Hill, is particularly noted for its antique stores, arts and crafts shops and speciality boutiques shown *above, and above and below left.* Situated close to Quincy Market the store *right* sells a variety of fresh fish, whilst the Union Oyster House *below* is the city's oldest restaurant.

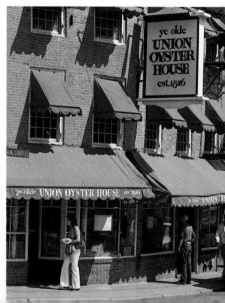

FRESHLY BOILED LOBS
FRESH CRAB F

SOFT SHELL
CRABS
JUMBO 1.89 RAINBOW 3.99 RED SNAPPER
SMELTS lb. TROUT lb.

CRAB 4.95
FLAKES lb.

Fresh Cape Native
BLUEFISH 1.98

FRESH
MUSSEL 3.98

FRESH NATIVE
MACKEREL 1.19

FINNAN HADDIE

Fresh Native
SWORDFISH $5.99 lb.

Extra Large
SHRIMP $6.99 lb.

CAPE $6.49
lb.

FRESH CAPE
BLUEFISH Fillets $3.49
lb.

0.95

Included in Boston's many cultural and historic attractions are The Museum of Science *above* and the U.S.S. Frigate "Constitution" *right and centre left*, restored and rebuilt in 1833 and known as "Old Ironsides". Commuter traffic can be seen at North Station *below left;* cars cross the Northern Avenue Bridge over Fort Point Channel *below*, whilst sunset floods the Longfellow Bridge, spanning the Charles River Basin, *above left.*

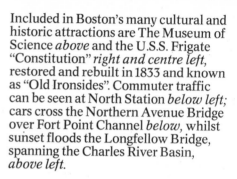

Forming a green and flowering oasis in the heart of the city, the Public Garden *above left* is particularly famous for its Swanboats *above and centre left,* and monuments to great men of the Republic, such as the equestrian statue of George Washington *right,* created by Thomas Ball. Pictured *overleaf* is the glittering city skyline along the Charles River, its peaceful riverbank equally as charming by day *below left.*

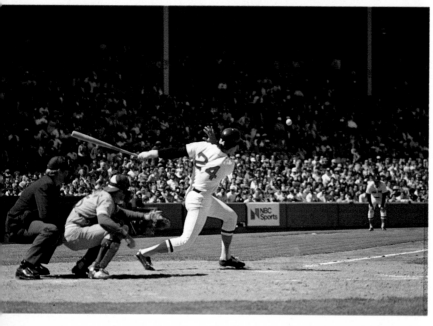

Bostonians take an exceptional interest in sport and with four major-league teams, three of which are championship winners, they are justly proud of their sporting achievements.
The Red Sox baseball team, who have twice won the coveted pennant, are featured *on these pages* at their headquarters in Fenway Park.

Further views of Boston's Public Garden pictured *on these pages and overleaf* reveal the tranquil charm of this lovely century-old park, with its flowering cherry blossom and banks of tulips.

Boston Common, site of the Soldiers and Sailors Monument *above left*, is also the location, each May Day, of the Annual Loyalty Day Programme illustrated *on these pages* when the Ladies Auxiliary to the Veterans of the Foreign Wars of the U.S. dedicate their allegiance to the democratic traditions of liberty and justice.

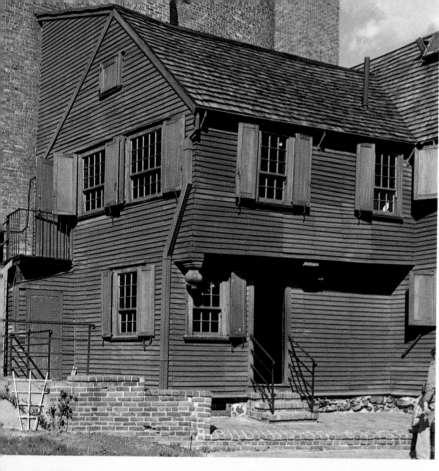

The Paul Revere House *above left*, situated at North Square, was purchased by the master silversmith in 1770 and is the oldest wooden structure in Boston. Its delightful interior *above, left and right*, is filled with many original furnishings. Sited in a tiny park at James Rego Square is the statue of Paul Revere *below*, which commemorates his famous horseback ride on the night of April 18th 1775, when he warned the city's residents of the invading Redcoats.

Shimmering lights add a magical quality to the city by night as they play along the tranquil water of the Charles River *below* and the plaza adjoining the Christian Science Church Center *above*. The gleaming John Hancock Tower can be seen *left*, whilst lamplight fills the deserted city street *right*.

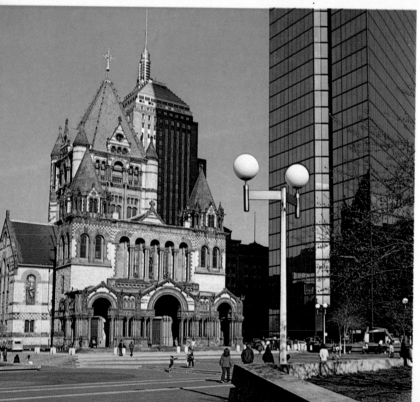

Reflected in the glossy exterior of the John Hancock Tower, Trinity Church *left*, located in historic Copley Square, is considered to be an outstanding example of Neo-Romanesque architecture and was created by Henry Hobson Richardson. Shown *right* is the interior of this magnificent church, with its panelled ceiling *below* and main altar *above* behind which is a series of exquisite stained-glass windows.

Boston contains a wealth of beautiful churches and some of its loveliest are featured on these pages. *Top right* is shown the Old South Church; *top left* the graceful interior of King's Chapel, the oldest Anglican Church in New England; *below right* the interior of the Christian Science Church Center, and *top centre and below* the Old North Church (Christ Church), of Paul Revere fame. The Old South Meeting House *below left,* once housed the congregation of the Third Church of Boston and is now a unit of the Boston Historical Park. *Overleaf* can be seen the Main Hall of the city's Museum of Science.

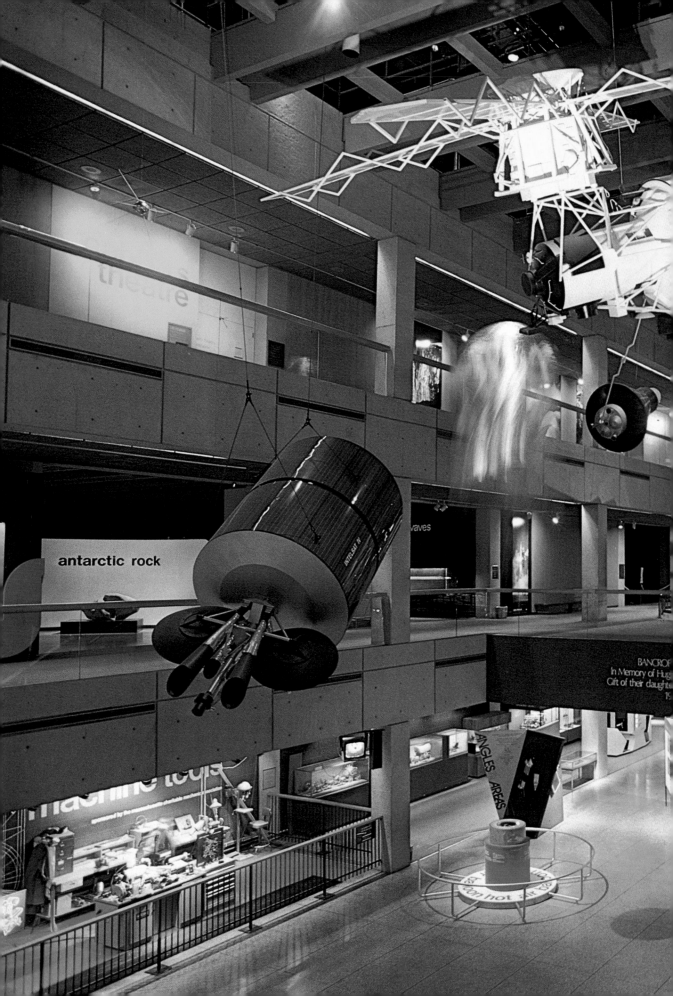

Founded in 1636, Harvard University is America's oldest institution of higher learning. Its complex of graduate and professional schools, including the Science Centre *above* and the Chemistry Building, behind which is sited the Alexander Calder Stabile *below*, line both sides of the Charles River. *Overleaf* can be seen Harvard Yard, the original centre of the college and *right* the Memorial Church. Boston Public Library *left*, completed in 1895, is one of the largest and finest libraries in the country.

Within the magnificent State House, designed by Charles Bulfinch in 1795, can be seen the Senate Chamber *below left*, and the marble-floored Memorial Hall *above left*, with its exquisite stained-glass ceiling *below*, whilst *above and right* is shown the impressive House of Representatives, where above the panelled walls a series of paintings details important events in the momentous history of Massachusetts.

Boston's unique charm lies in its blend of old and new, where carefully preserved Colonial buildings are intermingled with the modern structures of contemporary America. The city's rich heritage is evidence in the Old West Church *above;* The Old Corner Bookstore *above left;* Newbury Street *centre left;* Trinity Church on Copley Square *below left* and the Old South Meeting House on Washington Street *bottom.*

Beyond the gleaming skyscrapers along the waterfront shimmers the Dome of the State House *above right,* whilst *right* can be seen the tranquil scene near Commercial Wharf, where the children's playground *above* is also located.

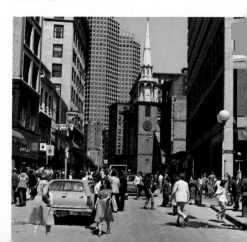

Marking the location of the famous battle which was fought on June 17th 1775, is the 221 feet high granite column of the Bunker Hill Monument *above*, whilst the statue *below*, commemorating Benjamin Franklin, fronts the old City Hall. The Museum of Fine Arts *above left* ranks amongst the greatest in the world: its comprehensive collections including those of Chinese and Indian Art, Greek and Roman sculpture and textiles and prints. Located directly opposite to the State House *right* is the monument *below left*, dedicated to Robert Gould Shaw and the black 54th Regiment which he led in the Civil War. Seen at sunset *overleaf*, the Charles River gleams like a broad, gold ribbon.

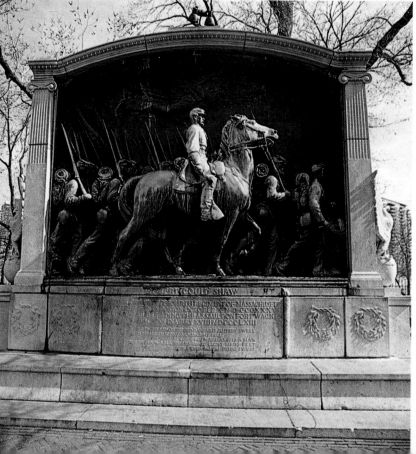

First published in 1979 by Colour Library International Ltd.
© Illustrations: Colour Library International (U.S.A.) Ltd, 163 East 64th Street, New York 10021.
Colour separations by La Cromolito, Milan, Italy.
Display and filmsetting by Focus Photoset, London, England.
Printed in Spain by Grijelmo, S. A.
Published by Crescent Books, a division of Crown Publishers Inc.
Library of Congress Catalogue Card No. 79-87535
CRESCENT 1979